Jake the Snake

Written and Illustrated
by Shelley Davidow

Jalmar Press

ISBN 978-1-931061-47-6

Jalmar Press
PO Box 370
Fawnskin, CA 92333
(800) 429-1192
F: (909) 866-2961
www.jalmarpress.com

About the Author and Illustrator: Shelley Davidow is originally from South Africa. Her young adult book, *In the Shadow of Inyangani,* was nominated for the first African Writer's Prize by Macmillan/Picador and BBC World. The author of numerous books, Shelley lives in Florida (USA), where she is a class teacher at the Sarasota Waldorf School.

About the Readers: These early readers are phonetically based and contain stories that young children will find enjoyable and entertaining. Each story has a beginning, middle and an ending. The stories are gently humorous while honoring nature, animals and the environment.

The six books use simple words that the early reader will easily grasp. They have been carefully chosen by a reading specialist to help students advance from the short vowels, to the silent "e", to the vowel combinations. At the back of this book is a list of sight words that should be reviewed with the child before reading the book.

About our Reading Specialist: Mary Spotts has been a remedial reading teacher for over ten years, taking countless classes and seminars to keep current in the field she loves. Her deep under-standing that struggling readers need good stories — particularly if the books are phonetically based — has been an inspiration in the creation of these books. Mary has been a constant guide, ensuring that the books address specific phonetic principles while retaining a gently humorous story line.

Mary's desire to have available meaningful children's stories with decodable words and Shelley's creative talents and love of literature have been the incentive and encouragement to bring these books to production.

For Merik

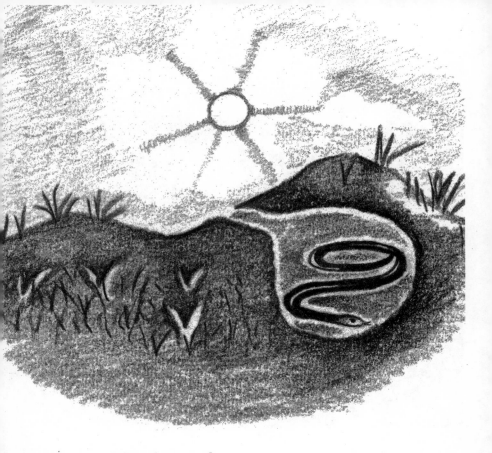

ake was a black snake.

He made a hole in the sand.

"This is my home," he said and went inside.

It was so soft and so snug that Jake had a nap.

Jake the Snake woke up.

He saw a nose in his soft, snug home.

He said, "I do not like a nose in my home."

The nose said, "I am not just a nose.
I am a mole, a mole with a nose.
My name is Mike."

"I do not like moles," said Jake the Snake.
Mike the Mole said, "I do not like snakes,
but I am lost. This is not a mole hole.
A mole hole is big. This is a snake hole."

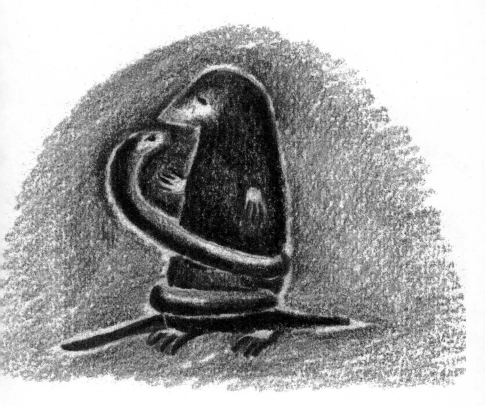

ıke the Snake slid to Mike the Mole.

 do not like moles in my soft, snug hole," he said.

But you are lost, so I will take you home."

Jake the Snake and Mike the Mole
left the snake hole in the sand.
They went to find a mole hole.

Mike the Mole said, "I am so glad
that you are not a bad or rude snake."
He and Jake went for a time.
Then they came to a hole in the sand.

Mike the Mole said, "This is my home!
A mole hole is not like a snake hole.
A mole hole is big and wide.
Moles like big, wide holes in the sand."

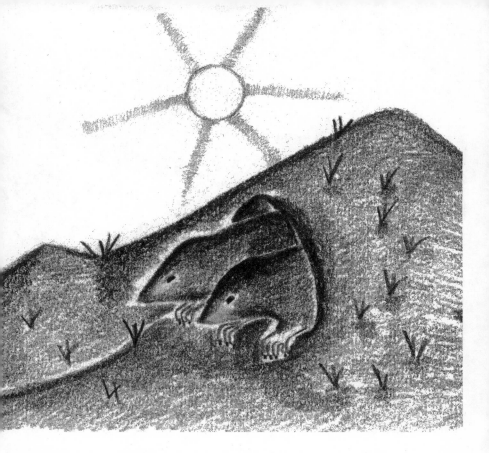

Mike the Mole went into his home.
Then he came back with his wife.
Mike had a fine wife.

Mike's wife said, "Jake the Snake, you are not a
bad snake. You are not a rude snake.
But do you like moles?"

Jake the Snake said, "I did not like moles.
But I like Mike the Mole, and I like you.
So, yes, I do like moles, I do!"

  11

Mike the Mole and his wife were glad.
They went into their mole hole.
Jake the Snake slid home.

Jake the Snake got home.
He went into his snake hole.
It was a snug home.

Jake the Snake had a soft, snug home.
It was a fine home for a fine, black snake.

14

Short Vowel Sounds

a	e	i	o	u
am	yes	it	lost	but
bad	left	is		snug
glad		this		
nap		will		
that		with		
sand				
black				

Silent "e" Sounds

a – e	i – e	o – e	u - e
take	like	nose	rude
made	Mike's	woke	
came	wide	holes	
name	wife	homes	
Jake	fine	moles	
snakes	inside		
	time		

Sight Words

said
my
to
do
you
I
are
find
were
their

CPSIA information can be obtained
at www.ICGtesting.com
Printed in the USA
BVHW030028070319
541987BV00001B/4/P